古琉球の武備を考察して「からて」の発達に及ぶ

THE ORIGIN OF KARATE

OR

OBSERVATIONS REGARDING THE DEVELOPMENT OF KARATE FOUND IN RECORDS OF THE OLD RYUKYU KINGDOM

WRITTEN BY: IHA FUYU (1876~1947)

TRANSLATED BY: ERIC SHAHAN

ISBN: 978-1-950959-87-7

THE ORIGIN OF KARATE

Translator's Note: A Brief Timeline of Karate in Ryukyu

Works with an asterisk (*) have been translated by Eric Shahan.

240 China's *Records of the Three Kingdoms* 三國志 tells of an envoy from China visiting mainland Japan for the first time. He describes both the land and people.

538 Introduction of Buddhism to Japan

629 China's *Book of Sui* 隋書, the *Account of the State of Ryukyu* 流求国伝 is compiled. This is the first appearance of the name Ryukyu 琉球 in an official historical text.

800 Local chieftains called Aji 按司 appear. They construct Gusuku 城 castles to guard their coasts.

1187 Shunten 舜天 the legendary first king of Chuzan, Central Mountain Kingdom, ascends the throne.

1296 The Mongol-led Yuan 元 dynasty of China sends 6,000 troops to invade Ryukyu, but the attempt ends in failure.

1314 Around this time, the Sanzan "Three Mountain" Era begins. The three rival states are: Central Mountain, Southern Mountain and Northern Mountain.

1349 Satto 察度 becomes King of Central Mountain.

1372 King Satto enters into tributary relations with Ming China. According to the *History of Ming* 明史, envoys are sent to Ryukyu. The first cultural and martial exchanges are thought to have begun. Chinese families settled near Shuri Castle, influencing later traditions.

1392 The Thirty-six families from Min, a group of Chinese bureaucrats and craftsmen emigrate to the Ryukyu Kingdom. They bring many Chinese administrative methods and texts such as Bubishi 武備志 influencing local martial traditions.

1404 With the death of King Satto, the first investiture envoy from China is dispatched to Ryukyu to confirm the new king.

1429 Sho Hashi unifies the three Mountain Kingdoms and the Ryukyu Kingdom is founded.

1432 Weapons such as spears, swords and armor are imported from Japan into Ryukyu.

1466 A Ryukyuan envoy astonishes people in Kyoto by firing guns during departure confirming that firearms are used in Ryukyu.

1467 The Onin War begins on mainland Japan, signaling the start of the warring states period, lasting until around 1600.

1470 King Sho En crowned king, beginning the Second Sho Dynasty which lasts until 1879.

1479 *Records in the Joseon Annals* describe Ryukyuan royal processions and weaponry, including firearms.

1501 First ban on weapons by King Sho Shin leading to the flourishing of unarmed fighting techniques.

1531 The first volume of Omoro Soshi おもろさうしpoems is compiled.

1553 Naha harbor is fortified with castles and cannon batteries.

1560 Seki Keiko publishes *New Treatise on Military Efficiency* 紀效新書 which includes illustrated explanations of thirty-two Kenpo techniques.

1607 Chinese official and Shorinji Kenpo practitioner Chin Genpin (1587~1671) travels to Japan. He made his way to Edo and took up temporary abode in Kokushoji Temple. Three Ronin, Fukuno Shichiro Uemon, Isome Jiro Saemon and Miura Oku Jiemon were also there and they asked him about his Shorinji Temple Kenpo. Chin taught them and the three Samurai included these teachings in their martial arts.

1609 With the permission of the Tokugawa Shogun, Satsuma domain invades Ryukyu. King Sho Nei surrenders at Shuri Castle. Ryukyu becomes a vassal nation of Satsuma Domain, though its status regarding China remains unchanged as Satsuma wants to profit from this trade.

1612 In China, Bo Genki 茅元儀 compiles the *Bubishi* 武備志 which includes most of Seki Keiko's *New Treatise on Military Efficiency*, including the drawings of Kenpo techniques.

1654 Peasants are prohibited from moving to urban centers such as Shuri, Tomari and Naha.

1727 The Qing Dynasty issued a ban on martial arts. The Shaolin Temple is burned down and the Shaolin monks move to Jiangnan.

1762 Tobe Yoshihiro writes *Oshima Hikki* 大島筆記 *Record of Oshima Island.* He describes a martial art that has well-developed footwork and a stance with one hand extended and the other on the chest.

1782 Sakugawa Chikagami Kanga (~1837) also known as "Karate Sakugawa" is born. He learns Kenpo from a Chinese military officer.

1790 Emissaries from Ryukyu travel to Edo to offer congratulations to Tokugawa Ienari.

1800 Matsumura Sokon (1798?~1892?) is born in Shuri. He practices Karate and Jigen Ryu Bojutsu. His wife was Tsuru was also a Karate practitioner. In a posthumous letter from 1873, he wrote,

In the way of martial arts, there three types of Budo, martial arts. Scholarly martial arts, martial artists in name only and martial artists actually doing martial arts.

1816 The British ships arrive in Ryukyu. Captain Basil Hall later writes *Voyage of Exploration to the Western Coast of Korea and the Great Ryukyu Islands* describing how the people of Ryukyu, while unarmed, would adopt a fighting stance,

On returning to the cabin to tea, they were all in high spirits, and while amusing themselves with a sort of wrestling game, Ookooma (a Ryukyu man,) *who had seen us placing ourselves in sparring attitudes, threw himself suddenly into the boxer's position of defense, assuming at the same time a fierceness of look which we had never before seen in any of them.*

The gentleman to whom he addressed himself, thinking that Ookooma wished to spar, prepared to indulge him; but Madera's quick eye saw what was going on, and by a word or two made him instantly resume his wonted sedateness. We tried in vain to make Madera explain what were the magical words which he had used to calm Ookooma.

Shiba Kokan (1738~1818) dies. His painting *Picture of a Wedding Banquet* 婚礼酒宴之図 shows what appears to be Ryukyu Karate.

1818	Shiba Kokan (1738~1818) dies. His painting *Picture of a Wedding Banquet* shows what appears to be Ryukyu Karate.
1829	Asato Anko born. (~ 1906) Later teaches Karate to Funakoshi Gichin.
1831	Itosu Anko born. (1831~1916) Starting around 1905 he begins working as a teacher in Shuri.
1850	Satsuma Domain Samurai Nagoya Sagenta (1820~1881) is banished to Amami Oshima for taking part in a household succession fight. The other participants were ordered to commit Seppuku. While on Oshima, he begins to record the life and folklore of the island including illustrations of Kenpo Jutsu and Makiwara. This book is published as *Various Tales of the Southern Isles.*
	Publication of 琉球入貢紀略 *Abridged Account Of Ryukyuans Visiting Japan To Pay Tribute*
1853	Commodore Perry's American fleet arrived in Japan. That year, Kanryo Higashionna (~1915) was born in Naha.
1866	Kentsu Yabu (~1937) born in Shuri Yamakawa. He later becomes a physical education instructor and also a lieutenant in the army. In March 1921, he presides over a Karate demonstration for the Crown Prince by his students at Shuri Castle. Funakoshi Gichin assisted him. In 1927, he gives a Karate demonstrations in Hawaii and Los Angeles.
1868	First year of the Meiji Restoration. Funakoshi Gichin (~1957) born in Shuri.
1870	Motobu Choki (~1944) born in Shuri
1872	The Meiji Government changes Ryukyu from a kingdom to a Domain, offically making it part of Japan.
1876	Iha Fuyu born in Naha (~1947)

1879	Ryukyu Domain abolished and Okinawa Prefecture is established. King Sho Tai surrenders Shuri Castle and moves to Tokyo.
1888	Chojun Miyagi (~1953) founder of Goju Ryu born in Naha. Served as Karate Instructor to the Okinawan Police.
1889	Mabuni Kenwa (~1952) born in Shuri. In 1929, he opened a dojo in Tsurumi, Osaka.
1893	Ryukyu Shinpo Newspaper begins publication
1894	First Sino-Japanese War (1894~1895)
1901	The last Ryukyu King Sho Tai dies (1843~1901)
1904	Russo-Japanese War (1904~1905)
1911	Iha Fuyu publishes *Ancient Ryukyu* considered to be the best work on Okinawan studies. On mainland Japan Judo and Kendo are adopted as regular subjects in middle schools and normal schools.
1912	Death of the Meiji Emperor and beginning of the Taisho Era. First Fleet calls at Nakagusuku Bay. Around a dozen officers disembark to train Karate at the Okinawa Prefectural First Junior High School.
1916	Funakoshi Gichin gives his first public karate demonstration at the Kyoto Butokuden.
1913	Ryukyu Shinpo Article: *Karate is the Essence of Martial Arts** by Funakoshi Gichin
1914	Ryukyu Shinpo Article: *The Martial Arts of Okinawa* * by Funakoshi Gichin

1921 On March 6th, Crown Prince Hirohito, en route to Europe, watches a Karate demonstration at the main hall of Shuri Castle.

1922 Funakoshi Gichin publishes Ryukyu Kenpo Karate.
The first Sports Exhibition sponsored by the Ministry of Education is held in Tokyo. Funakoshi Gichin and Gima Shinkin give karate demonstrations. Both are later invited by Kano Jigoro to demonstrate at his Dojo. Funakoshi demonstrates Kanku Dai and Gima demonstrates Naifanchi. Afterwards, Funakoshi stays in Tokyo, residing at the Meisho Juku dormitory.

1924 Funakoshi Gichin issues the first ever dan ranks in Karate.
Public Physical Education Resources Magazine article:*
Ryukyu Kenpo Karate
By Funakoshi Gichin

1925 In September, the magazine King features an article about Motobu Choki defeating a foreign boxer, but uses an illustration of Funakoshi.

1926 Motobu Choki publishes *Okinawan Kenpo Karate Jutsu: Kumite**

1932 Motobu Choki publishes *My Karate Jutsu**

1932 Iha Fuyu publishes *The Origin of Karate** in honor of Funakoshi Gichin's sixtieth birthday. He also publishes *A Study of Military Force and Magic in Ryukyu History*

1934 Mabuni Kenwa publishes *Karate Kenpo The Art of Self Defense** as well as *Karate Kenpo: Training Seipai**

1935 Funakoshi Gichin publishes *Karate-do Kyohan*

1937 Pen Magazine article:
*Karatedo and the Japanese Spirit**
By Funakoshi Gichin

1939 Shotokan Dojo opens.

	Funakoshi Gichin's third son, Funakoshi Gigo, publishes an article in Taiso magazine *What is Karate?**
1941	Pacific War begins. Public Discussion Magazine article: *The Story of Karatedo** By Funakoshi Gichin
1944	Motobu Choki dies at the age of 74
1945	Pamphlet *National Resistance Manual* 国民抗戦必携 is published which encourages citizens to resist the impending allied ground invasion by, *...making use of the striking and grappling techniques particular to the martial arts of Japan, such as those found in Judo or Karate.* *
1946	Funakoshi Gichin's son Funakoshi Gigo dies at the age of 39 (1906~1945)
1947	Iha Fuyu dies at the age of 71
1951	Funakoshi Gichin publishes *Karatedo Nyumon*
1952	Mabuni Kenwa dies at the age of 62
1956	Funakoshi Gichin publishes *Karatedo: My Path**
1957	Funakoshi Gichin dies at the age of 89

Translator's Introduction

Iha Fuyu 伊波普猷 (1876~1947) was a Japanese scholar who studied Ryukyu and Okinawan culture, customs, linguistics, and folklore. Iha, considered to be the father of Okinawaology, was born in Naha into a low-ranked Samurai household. Iha enrolled at University of Tokyo in 1903 and dedicated himself to the study of the Ryukyu languages, folklore and history. He also researched Ryukyu traditions with Funakoshi Gichin, founder of the Shotokan Karate School

This was the first time that an Okinawan language meeting was held within the Ryukyu Asahi Company. Folklorist Yanagita Kunio was also in attendance at the meeting that was held last month (June) on the 29th.
Some of those who come from the Loocho (Ryukyu) Islands met together at the Tokyo Asahi recently. Photo shows the attendants on that day.
The Asahi Graph Magazine July 13, 1927 issue

Members of the Southern Isles Discussion Group 南島談話会 Front row third from right is Fuyu Iha and on his right is Funakoshi Gichin. On the far right in the front row is Yanagita Kunio.

In 1911 Iha published *Ko Ryukyu* 古琉球 *Ancient Ryukyu,* considered the most authoratative book on the origins of the Ryukyu people and their traditions. Iha Fuyu died in Tokyo in 1947 at the age of 71.

Regarding the Translation:

Iha first published *The Origins of Karate* in Showa 7 (1932) and the study was later included in *A Literary Collection Commemorating the Sixtieth Birthday of Funakoshi Gichin Sensei* 富名腰義珍先生還暦記念詩文集 published in 1933. Later, it was also published in *Shima* 島 *Island* Magazine (focusing on Okinawa) in the same year as well as in *Monthly Karatedo* 月間空手道 in 1956.

Iha Fuyu in his study

There were no images in this book, all have been added by the translator.

All brackets except for ones with birth and death dates of persons mentioned are by the author.

Former head of the Okinawa Prefectural Library Iba Fuyu

古琉球の武備を考察して「からて」の発達に及ぶ

THE ORIGIN OF KARATE

OR

OBSERVATIONS REGARDING THE DEVELOPMENT OF KARATE FOUND IN RECORDS OF THE OLD RYUKYU KINGDOM

IHA FUYU
1932

The Origin of Karate

At the beginning of the fourteenth century, according to the Western calendar (around 1314~1335,) the largest of Japan's southern isles, Okinawa Island, was divided into the Central Mountain, Southern Mountain and Northern Mountain kingdoms. A great number of horrific battles played out as each of these three kingdoms vied with the others to increase their power and territory. However, a man named Sho Hashi (1372~1439) emerged and began to gain power.

He was from a region in Southern Mountain (nowadays known as Shimajiri Region.) In 1409 he overthrew and destroyed the armies of the Middle Mountain Kingdom, establishing the first Sho Kingdom. Over the next twenty-five years, he put an end to all the various regional squabbles that had been flaring up over the past hundred years.

Since the best port on the island, Naha, was located in Middle Mountain, trade flourished between Ryukyu, China, Japan, Korea as well as barbarian nations to the south. This meant the Sho Kingdom rapidly solidified its economic base. One clear benefit was adopting more advanced foreign weaponry, and it hardly needs stating that the king quickly used this military advantage to subjugate the northern and southern mountain kingdoms. However, the defeated lords were dissatisfied with their treatment at the hands of the victors, and after the death of Hashi the prosperity of the past sixty-six years collapsed into civil war as the various warlords sought to increase their territory.

In this period of revolution, a Ryukyu civil official named Kanemaru (King Sho En) (1415~1476) who was from Iheyai Island. This time the new government lasted through the period where Toyotomi's rule of the whole of Japan passed to Tokugawa.

And with that over a hundred and twenty years of civil war came to an end. This era was often referred to as *Ikusa Hana Asobi,* "the beautiful flowering of violence during war play." During that time great military tacticians like Sho Hashi and Gosamaru emerged, and battle strategies were refined and perfected.

This may seem to jump ahead in the story a bit, however I would like to discuss the placement and construction of the support castles in the Central Mountain and Southern Mountain areas. So, I will put aside the discussion of the former for now and briefly outline the latter. The north wall of Shuri is from the early modern era and dates to the fourteenth year of Seitoku (1519) in the Ming Dynasty. The stone gate of Sonohyan-utaki was designed and built by stone smith Nishito of Takeshima in the Yaeyama Island group. It seems clear that it was built in the early fifteenth century. According to Matsunaga Hisahide, this stone gate was built forty-five years before the early modern era style Shigayama Castle was built in the third year of Eiroku (1560.) Further, it was built ninety years before Nakajo Castle, which was done in the same style and served as the place where Commodore Perry astonished everyone with his arrival (This is the main castle of Gosamaru, a map of which is included in Commodore Perry's Account of His Invasion.) Professor Higashionna believes it is much older than Ue Castle on Kume Island.

It goes without saying that the people of these islands who built castle also used bladed weapons. In the twenty first volume of *Omoro Soshi* (Kume Island no Omoro,) which should perhaps be considered the Manyoshu of Ryukyu contains the following passage in chapter fifty-three, describing an Omoro.[1] The song is as follows,

Red scabbard, handle and hand guard of my sword
The fittings of the highest quality
Have formed a clever plan, We attack

A glorious action!
First group moves forward

Second group moves forward
Wearing an iron helm bright as gold!

Armor strapped on my body
A beautiful Ushidate shield in on hand
A halberd with a lacquered handle in the other!

Attacking the wooden gate
Attacking the iron gate!

It is pretty clear that from the third line of the first stanza on down

---

[1] *Omoro* is a traditional story-song in Ryukyu. These story-songs are in a Ryukyu language, however there are some Japanese words as well. There are said to be six Ryukyu languages.

is meant to be sung and that the remaining stanza are as well. The words for helm, armor, Ushidate shield and lacquered halberd are obviously Japanese words. From this we can determine that the Ryukyu people imported Japanese weapons to their islands across the vast seas, much as they do today.

There are also Omoro, ancient remembrances written as poem-songs,[2] from as early as the Heian era (794~1185) that talk about the Ryukyu people travelling to Yamato (mainland Japan) to purchase the teardrop shaped Magatama jade pieces and other goods. Reading such songs, one can readily understand and accept that such exchanges already existed.[3]

What follows is a song that dates to the final year of the first King of Ryukyu.[4] It was thought to have been sung as the King's forces chased off the Shoren army that had surrounded Shuri castle. The song (chapter 15 of the tenth volume) is as follows,

Samurai of Shuri
Elite Warriors, brave and stalwart,
Truly you should be considered invincible,
Amongst all the warriors in the castle,
You are the elite, brave and stalwart,
Select your sword and fasten it to your hip,
Select your armor and strap it on,
On the slope of Nema you felled seventy men,
On Giho Slope you fell a hundred men

---

[2] The oldest and most famous collection of these poem-songs is the *Omoro Soshi* おもろさうし *Collection of Omoro Songs* which was compiled under the direction of the Ryukyu King. It contains Omoro from the 16th~17th centuries.

[3] The use of Magatama in trade started in the Jomon Era (14,000~300 BC) Made of agate, jade, crystal, amber, glass, etc.

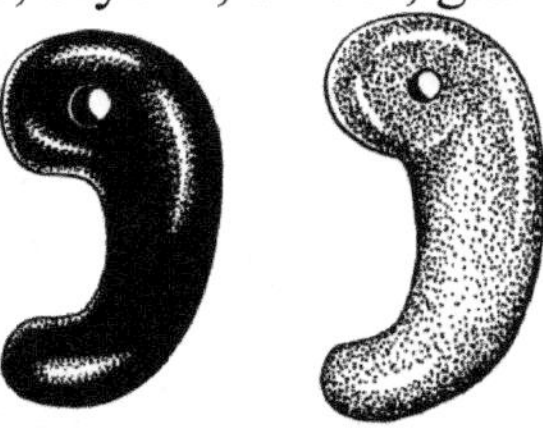

[4] Sho Hashi 尚巴志(1372 ~ 1439) is traditionally described as the unifier of Okinawa and the founder of the Ryukyu Kingdom.

This is the way of the men of Shuri
This is the way of those serving at the King's castle
To the King of Shuri Banzai!
To the King in Shuri Castle Banzai!

That is the story-song. Clearly the second line would be repeated after each following line. From this story we learn that it was not just generals that wore armor into combat, but common soldiers as well. Volume seven contains the following,

Shuri ten-giyasuhe anshi osoi ganashi hai no Omoro Soshi
Shuri, protected by heaven and guarded by the noble lord, flourishes.

When I was young,
I chose and took up precious jewels.
But now, having reached a hundred years of age,
I heap up gold and present it,
and stand in attendance before my lord.
When I was young,
I chose armor and put it on.

What this song describes is a young man choosing a sword to wear on his hip. However now that he has passed the age of seventy, he wears brocade garments and serves at his King's side.[5] In other words, as a youth this warrior selected and wore armor. (When the song was sung, it seems the section from the fourth line on down was repeated.)[6]

This song was probably composed by an old general who, having achieved success and fame, sang it out of gratitude for the overwhelming and undeserved favor of the Ryukyu King.

---

[5] 人生七十古来 To reach seventy is rare since ancient times.

The author is referring to a line by the Chinese poet Du Fu (712~770 AD) who was celebrated for his moral vision and technical mastery.

[6] Brackets by the author.

Map of the Three Mountain Kingdoms (1322~1429)
and Major Castles

Furthermore, in Book Ten, Chapter Fourteen, there appears the line:

Momosowo Motarahe, Nasoyumi Motarahe
One hundred men carry armor, and seventy men carry bows

From this passage we know that bows were also used. The examples above come from the central part of the main island of Okinawa (known as Chuzan, Central Mountain.) However, in Chapter Forty-Five of Book Seventeen (the Omoro songs of Hokuzan, Northern Mountain), the terms "golden armor" and "golden halberds/spears" also appear.[7] In addition, in Book Twenty (the Omoro songs of Nanzan, Southern Mountain), Chapter Four, there is a Omoro song stating (in the remote southern extremity of Southern Mountain)

Kurokawa no Yoroi Migakase
People were polishing black leather armor

From this, it is clear that weapons and armor had already become widely distributed during the wars between the Three Mountain Kingdoms.

Moreover, in Book Thirteen (also from Chuzan, Central Mountain), Chapter Sixty-One, the phrase,

Kin Katchu Tsukuraete
Have golden armor made

From this, it seems clear that in this era Chuzan, the Central Mountain Kingdom, had developed the art of making armor.

[7] It is difficult to determine if the Kanji used refers to spears or halberds.

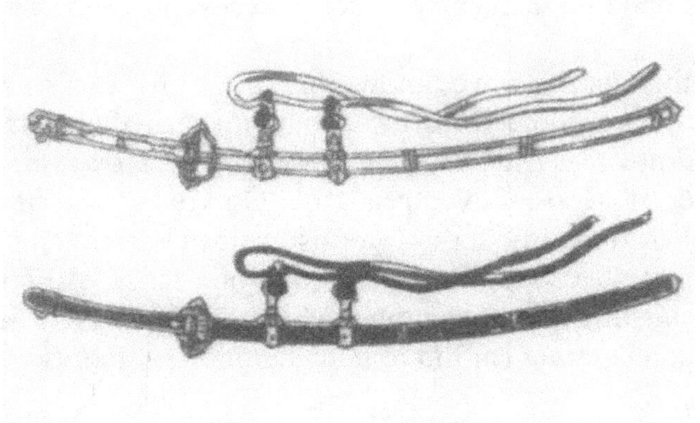

Tachi would have been hung from the belt, with the blade facing down. These swords were most effective when striking from horseback.

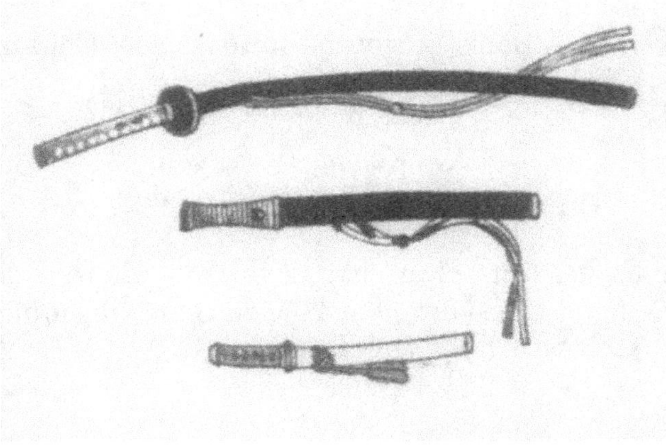

Koshi Gatana, also known simply as Katana were a backup sword.
Illustrations of Two Hundred Weapons 武器皕圖
Edo Era

Lord of Chibana, beautiful in face and bearing,
Lord of Chibana with the beautiful mouth,

Tie a Hachimaki headband tightly around his brow
Drape a Jinbaori battle surcoat over his shoulders,

Tie a silk belt around him,
Hang a Tachi long sword from his waist
Thrust a Koshi Gatana into his belt,

Tie sandals made of goatskin on his feet,
Give him a groom to attend his horse,
Place a golden saddle upon a white horse,

Paint an image of sun upon the front wheel,
On the back wheel paint the moon and send him forth.

That is roughly the meaning of the passage. From this we can see the typical way a warrior at the time would dress and equip themselves.

The above examples comes from a Omoro song, but it is perhaps necessary to supplement this with information from historical documents dating to that era.

紫瀾星極仰朝威萬里東來
貢獻時莫笑蠻邦尤蠢爾衣
冠猶見漢官儀
九州百變典刑空絕島猶能
見古風魋結殆臚鍬陋俗先
王鼓樂在其中
枕山大沼厚
中山王

中山王
英林

In the Korean official chronicle *Veritable Records of the Joseon Dynasty*,[8] Volume 105, under the entry for the 10th year of King Seongjong's reign (This is the 15th year of Chenghua in the Ming dynasty, or the 11th year of Bunmei in Japan and 1479 according to the Western calendar), June 10, there is a record stating that shipwrecked sailors from the Ryukyu Kingdom washed ashore on Jeju Island. Some of them were wearing gold hairpins. The court historians recorded what people reported having seen and heard.

> We happened to see the mother of the king of the country going out on an excursion. She rode in a lacquered palanquin with curtains hanging on all four sides. About twenty attendants accompanied her, all wearing garments of white ramie cloth and they covered their heads with silk fabric.[9]

---

[8] The *Veritable Records of the Joseon Dynasty* cover more than 470 years of the history of the dynasty, from 1392~1863.) With the kings as the central figures, the annals are daily records of the overall history and culture of the Joseon Dynasty, covering politics, military affairs, the social system, law, economics, industry, transportation, communications, customary arts, crafts, religion, etc.

One example entry:

> *Accession Year (1418), Month 8, Day 21, Entry 8 The Ryukyu envoy meets a storm The governor of Gyeongsang Province reported, "The Kingdom of Ryukyu dispatched an envoy with gifts to Joseon, but the envoy met a storm. His ship was damaged, and the gifts were swept away and lost. Over seventy persons drowned, and many of the survivors are sick or injured. Now the vessel has arrived and is moored at Hansan Island." The King ordered clothing and food bestowed on the survivors and that they be brought to the capital using the food and horses of post stations.*

[9] Illustrations on previous pages:
琉球入貢紀略 1850
Abridged Account Of Ryukyuans Visiting Japan To Pay Tribute

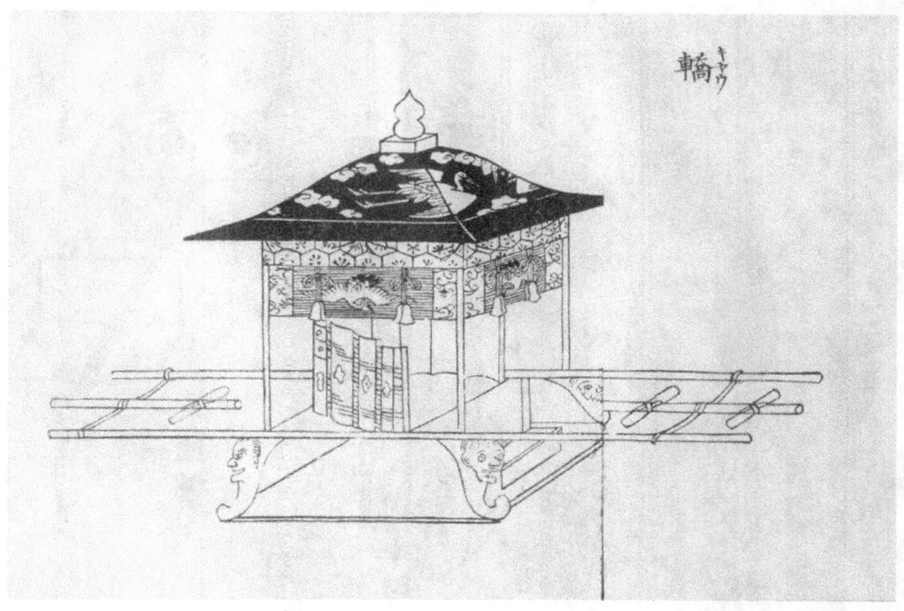

Ryukyu Palanquin

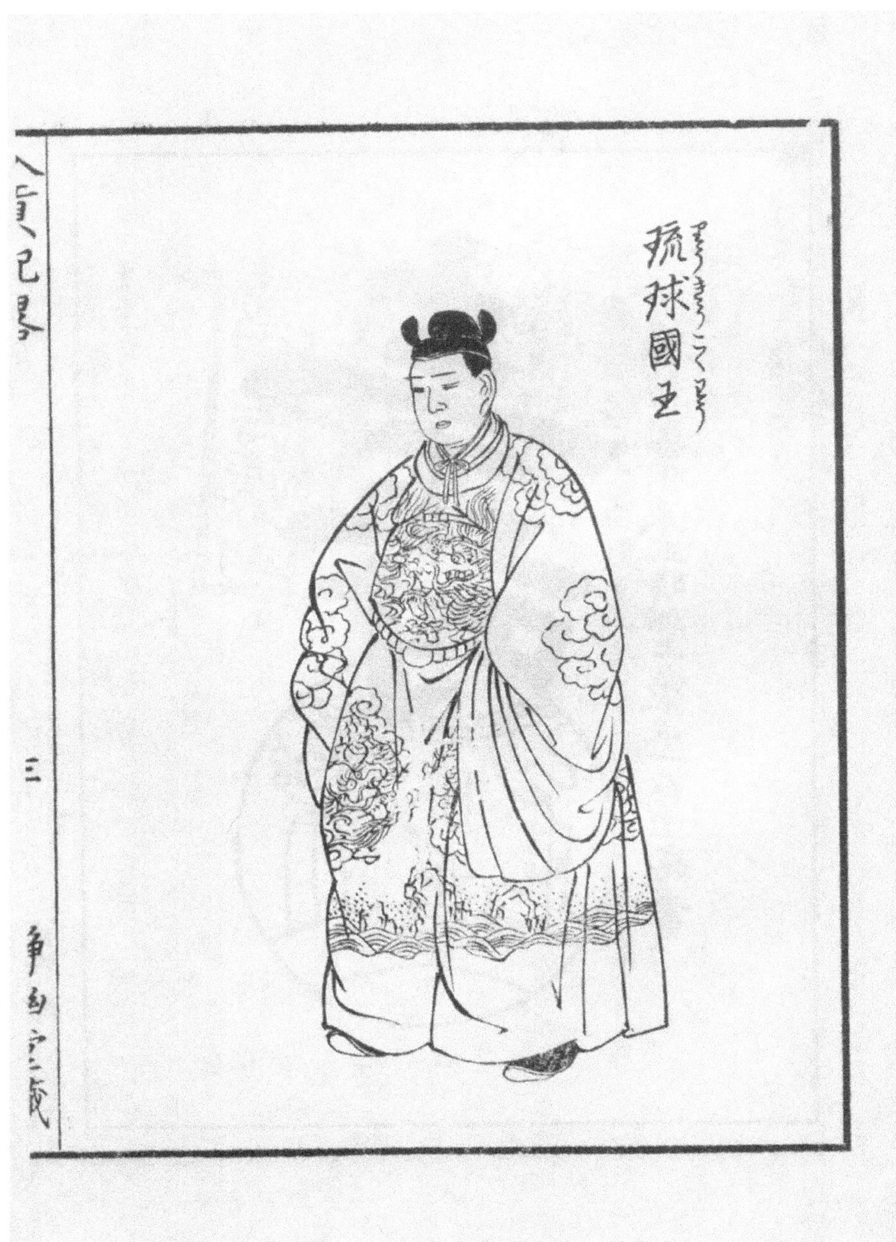

Ryukyu King

The passage continues,

> The soldiers, surrounding and guarding the procession, wore swords on their hips and carried bows and full quivers of arrows. Several hundred people surrounded and guarded the procession in front and behind. They blew horn trumpets and ceremonial flutes and discharged matchlocks. There were also four or five beautiful young women (the author may have mistaken the young men for women) wearing crimson silk garments, They wore long outer robes made of white ramie cloth. We went to the roadside and bowed in greeting.
>
> The palanquin halted, and they brought out Sake in two iron bottles and served it to us in lacquered wooden cups. Its taste was the same as the Sake of our own country.
>
> Three young boys came somewhat later by another route. They were a little over ten years old and very handsome in appearance. Their hair hung down behind so that it was difficult to distinguish whether they were male or female. They wore red silk garments with belts and rode well-fed horses. Those holding whips and attending them all wore white clothes.
>
> Four or five mounted riders rode ahead as guides. Many attendants accompanied them on both sides. More than twenty guards accompanied them, walking along while carrying long swords. Some attendants walked beside the horses holding umbrellas to shield the riders from the sun.
>
> We also bowed and paid respects to the young lord. He dismounted and poured us Sake from an iron bottle. After we finished drinking, he mounted his horse again and departed.
>
> The people of the country said that the king had died, and the heir was still young, therefore his mother governed the court on his behalf.
>
> When the young lord grows older, he will become the king. Furthermore, in this country there are weapons such as bows and arrows, axes, halberds, swords, spears, sickles, hooks and armor. Some of these weapons are made of iron, while others are made of leather.
>
> The armor worn by the soldiers had iron over the shins and some used leather to cover their knees. It resembled the leggings worn for travel.

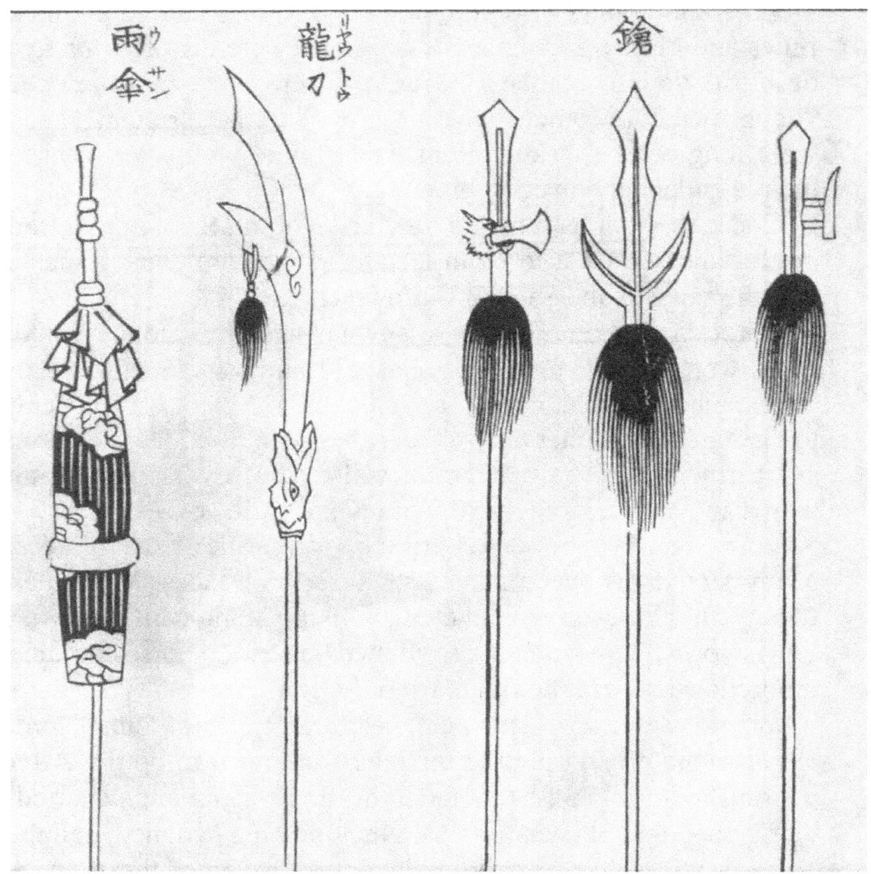

L: Usan – Rain Umbrella
C: Ryuto – Dragon Sword
R: Yari – Spears

This account regarding Samurai and warriors quoted above corresponds well with those found in the traditional Ryukyu Omoro songs.

This year was eleven years after the fall of the First Sho Dynasty (1406~1469,) and four years after the death of Sho En (1415 ~ 1476,) the founder of the Second Sho dynasty.[10] It was precisely the third year of King Sho Shin's reign.[11] The fact that the spirit of Ryukyu Warring States Period (1300s~ 1429) still lingered at that time can be seen from the practice of Junshi, following your lord in death.[12]

Although the country had become fairly peaceful, Japanese Wako pirates and other brigands occasionally attacked, so the nation could not completely disarm the populus. In the passage cited above, it is recorded that firearms were discharged along the road. It appears that the people of Ryukyu had long ago learned the use of gunpowder from the Chinese.

In the *Daily Record of Inryoken* the following entry appears:[13]

First year of Bunsho (1467) Seventh Month, Twenty-fifth day

> Officials of the Ryukyu Kingdom came, entered the court, and performed three bows before withdrawing. They then presented local products as tribute. When they withdrew, they fired two shots from firearms, as if there was an emergency. Everyone who heard the explosions was astonished.

This describes an event in the year before the outbreak of the Onin War, when Ryukyuan ambassadors visited the Muromachi Shogun. After being entertained, they took their leave, and at that time the

---

[10] There are two Sho Dynasty: the First (1429~1469) and Second (1470~1879.)

[11] 1477~1526 Sho Shin reigns; considered the "Golden Age," with expansion of trade, culture, and construction of temples and roads

[12] This is done even when a lord dies of old age or disease.

[13] *Inryoken Nichiroku* 陰涼軒日録 *Daily Record of Inryoken* is a diary kept by the monk Kikei Shinrui (1401~1469) who lived in Inryoken, a temple that was within the grounds of the Shokouji 相国寺 Buddhist Zen temple in Kyoto. Kikei recorded the affairs of the Ashikaga Shogun, temple ceremonies and foreign envoys from Ming China and Ryukyu.

blank shots caused considerable astonishment amongst the Japanese.

This is understandable. It was about a hundred and eighty years after the Mongol invasions, and seventy-eight years before firearms came into Japanese hands in the thirteenth year of Tenbun (1544?)[14]

According to *A Chronicle of Japan Volume Two*,[15] the loud blasts fired by the emissaries from Ryukyu sounded like a *Zudoon!* and was apparently a Ryukyu custom during ceremonies, so it may have been regarded as a kind of *Reiho*, honorific firing of a cannon or gun.[16]

---

[14] Iba Sensei placed a question mark here. Kublai Khan sent forces to conquer Japan in 1274 and 1281. The Mongol warriors surprised the Japanese Samurai (right) by fighting in groups (left) and using explosives (center.) Following these battles, Samurai changed tactics.

[15] *Zoku Honcho Tsugan* 続本朝通鑑 *A Chronicle of Japan Volume Two* describes historical events up to the 17th century.

[16] Illustration on the following page of a weapon similar to what was described. The gun is the "Five Thunder God Machine" fired by pulling the chain hanging from the right.
Bubishi 武備志 *Treatise on Armament Technology*
1621 Volume 125 (45)

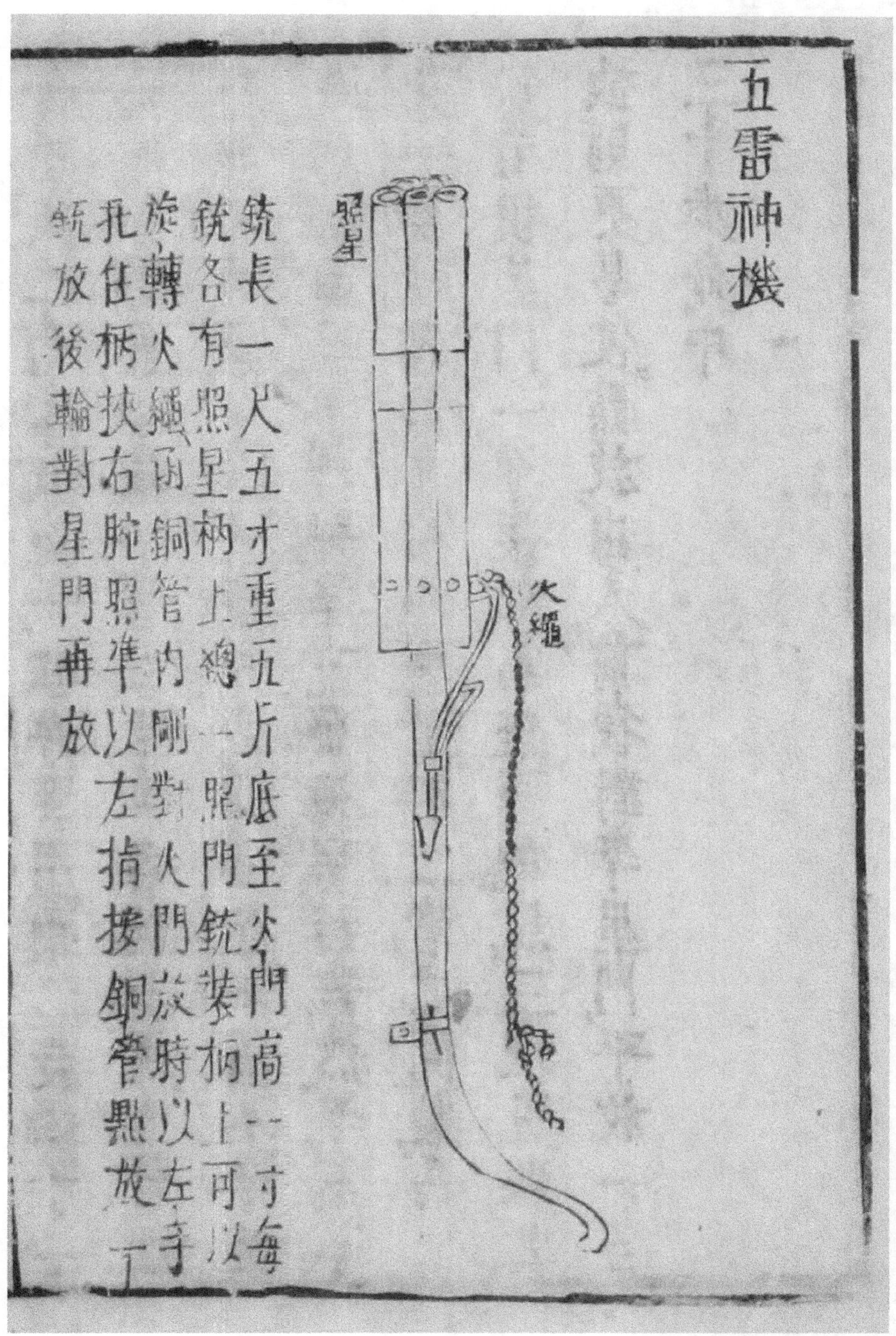

五雷神機

銃長一尺五寸重五斤底至火門高一寸每銃各有照星柄上總一照門銃裝柄上可以旋轉火繩面銅管內剛對火門放時以左手扎住柄扶右腕照準以左指撥銅管點放一銃放後輪對星門再放

Nakajima School Gunnery
Firing a Hiya

However, it was likely not a true firearm. Rather, it consisted of three iron tubes about 1 Sun, 1 inch, in diameter and roughly 60 Sun, 5 feet, long and bound together, with a handle about 6 Shaku, 6 feet, long attached. It was a device used even up to recent times, called a *Hiya,* fire-arrow. This was the year after King Sho Toku, the last ruler of the First Sho dynasty, returned in triumph from his campaign against Kikai Island.[17] However, it is not clear whether this type of projectile weapon was actually used in warfare at that time.

In the third year of the Hongzhi era of Ming China (1490,) thirteen years after Koreans and others had drifted ashore in Ryukyu, King Sho Shin, the third ruler of the second Sho Dynasty, sent people to Ming China to learn the method of "smoke-flower gunpowder" (this is referring to studying how to construct fireworks. In the Ryukyu language these are known as *Hihanachi.* This word most likely is the phonetic adaptation of the Chinese word *Huahuaxi* "fireworks display" into the Ryukyu language) or using gunpowder to make fireworks.[18] This is recorded in the official history *Kyuyo, Chronicle of Ryukyu*, compiled starting 1743, which states,

> Matsuji Hiyasedo, officer in charge of fire-arrow weapons, accompanied the tribute mission and, when entering Fujian and going to the capital, learned how to construct fireworks and returned.

---

[17] Sho Toku 尚徳 (1441~1469) was the son of Sho Taikyu, the first Sho King and was the last king of the First Sho Dynasty. In 1466, he led an invasion on Kikai Island, which strained the Ryukyuan treasury with little benefit. He either died young or was possibly killed by forces within the kingdom as details are somewhat unclear."

Boats rarely passed, and people were scared. Residents were dark colored and their words were incomprehensible. Men did not wear eboshi, and women did not wear their hair down. There were no farmers or grain, not even clothing. In the center of the island was a tall mountain, and it was constantly in flames. Due to the large amounts of sulfur, the island was also known as Sulfur Island.

-The Tale of the Heike
Translated by Burton Watson

[18] Smoke flower medicine 烟花薬

A note adds:

From this time onwards fireworks began in our country.

The title Hiyasedo, officer in charge of fire-arrow weapons, literally refers to the officer responsible for firearms or gunpowder weapons. Since this title appears to have existed from ancient times, we can conclude that weapons using gunpowder may have been used in warfare in this period.[19]

Next, let us look at the description of military mobilization around that time. The fifth chapter of the first book of Omoro Soshi (songs from the era of Sho Shin), contains the following,

Kikoe Ogimi
Putting on the red armor of dawn,
Advancing in order,
Resounding magnificently

(Also) palanquin
The august ruler resounds,
With the moon-white coiffure set in place

(Also)
The wise ones stand ready.

What this means is that when the Kikoe Ogimi, head priestess, dons her red armor and attaches a Tachi, long sword, to her belt, her presence reverberates across the entirety of the Ryukyu Kingdom. Full of sacred power and authority she walks forward. Ahead of her are the priestesses who serve the king, ahead of them are the sacred male attendants and the sacred female attendants.

The Kikoe Ogimi was the highest religious office in the kingdom, and the position was filled by one of the king's sisters. The Kikoe was regarded as the *Onari-gami*, the protecting spiritual counterpart of the king (the *Ikimi-tama* 生御魂 literally the living soul of the royal

---

[19] The title Hiyasedo is written 比屋勢頭 which phonetically writes fire arrow, normally written with Kanji that depict the literal meaning 火矢 (hiya) as 比屋 which are Ateji, Kanji that replicate the sound but do not have the same meaning. Sedo 勢頭 is officer in charge.

sister.)

In the Omoro songs, a word that means the same thing also appears: *Kuseserikiyo* (which refers to a mysterious person who can relay the will of the gods through words.)

Empress Jingu (169~ 269 AD) with her minister
By Katsukawa Shun'ei 1780s

It seems difficult to believe that in that era women actually went into battle clad in armor and carrying two swords like Empress Jingu. Therefore, this description cannot be understood unless another explanation is considered.

According to *Nyokan Ozoshi* 女官御双紙 *Record of the Court Women* published in the 1700s, in the 13th year of Koji (which was the twenty-fourth year of King Sho Shin's reign, or 1500), when Akahachi "Red Hornet" of the Yaeyama Islands raised a rebellion, *Kimi-Hae*, Goddess of the South Wind (a female priestess) was dispatched to Kume Island from the oracle office at Shuri.

It was said that if the priestess sent by Shuri arrived on the island, the Kami (God) of Kume island would naturally submit. If the Kami of the island submitted, the people would follow suit. Thus we see in this story that the *Kimi-Hae*, Goddess of the South Wind, led the army and the islands were re-conquered with relative ease.

Such stories can also be found in the *Kojiki* 古事記 *Records of Ancient Matters*, the first chronicle of Japan written in 711 AD. Moreover, since the tradition of *Kashima-dachi*, the god of war setting out from Kashima Shrine, people believed that if aid was called for, the war-god would go forth to the battlefield to offer protection.[20]

Even during the Russo-Japanese War, rumors circulated that the Hachiman god of war had ridden out to battle on a white horse from every shrine in every prefecture, or that the *Mikoshi,* shrine palanquins, stored at shrines had started rattling in the middle of the night as if seeking to be released to assist soldiers on the front.

In fact, in a letter dated January 30th of this year (1932) sent to the scholar of Ainu folklore, Kindaichi Kyosuke, from his younger brother living in Hizume Town of the Shiwa District in Iwate Prefecture. The following was written:

> Recently, every night the gods are setting off for Manchuria. Last night I saw three or four gods pass by on their way. Gods have been departing since around the end of last year, but for the past ten days or so it has been every night.
>
> Before, nothing happened until deep in the night, but lately the gods have begun drifting by playing Kagura music with flutes, drums and bells as early as nine or ten o'clock. As you know, there are many gods dwelling in the remote areas of Japan. Besides the prefectural and village shrines, every household has its own protective deity they worship, so there are many to send them off.
>
> Many of them are Makura-gami, gods that appear in people's dreams and when we consult the Miko, Shinto Maiden, she says that the gods wish to go to Manchuria.

---

[20] Kashima Shrine 鹿島神宮 is a Shinto shrine in Kashima, Ibaraki Prefecture. It is dedicated to Takemikazuchi-no-Okami 武甕槌大神 who answers the prayers of warriors.

> Inspired, the people of the neighborhood make preparations together, place the gods on horses, and escort them to Shigariwake Shrine (Shikinai Shrine, formerly the northernmost ancient shrine in the Tohoku area.)[21]

It is quite mysterious that even as the situation in Manchuria unfolds, such beliefs have remained almost unchanged from ancient times. Therefore, it is hardly remarkable if similar beliefs seem to have existed in the ancient Ryukyu Kingdom.

In addition, women in Ryukyu had long taken major roles in rituals. Ryukyu priestesses, beginning with the Kikoe Ogimi, High Priestess, and all the ones below, were regarded as divine beings. As the proverb states,

Onna wa Ikusa no Sakigake
Women are the ones who lead the first charge

This mean that in order to conquer your enemy, you must first subdue their deity.

In ancient times there were cases in which a sorcerer could utter a single spell and cause even a brave warrior to completely lose his strength and nerve. This kind of belief does not seem so strange if you understand the fact that primitive people, when faced with an obstacle they believed to be magical in origin, sometimes actually died from fright.

---

[21] When the author says "tie the gods to horses" they may be referring to sculptures or other reliquaries. This is an ancient shine first which functioned as an important regional shrine where such spiritual send-offs could occur. Shikinai Jinja 式内神社 is a shrine listed in the ancient government register compiled in 927.

罹仏祇在之殃者條〻子細如此
若雖為一事存曲折令違者
梵天帝釋四大天王惣日本國中
六十餘州大小神祇殊伊豆筥根
兩所權現三嶋大明神八幡大菩
薩天滿大自在天神部類眷屬神
罰冥罰各可罷蒙者也仍起請如件

Translator's Note: Hojo Yasutoki's Oath to the Gods

Should anyone violate the articles in this treaty, then all deities in Japan, great and small, and especially the great gods of Izusan, Hakone, and Mishima, together with Hachiman and Tenjin shall inflict terrible punishment upon them.

The "great gods" refers to the deities enshrined at the religious sites connected with the Kamakura era warriors:

Izusan Shrine
Hakone Shrine
Mishima Taisha

If we read the Omoro poem again, with these facts in mind, the scene in which a priestess of noble birth is clad in armor, wearing swords and advancing on the enemy under the protection of a guardian deity, with lower level priestesses going ahead, can be interpreted not as an actual military action but rather as a ritual performed before an army sets out for war. It was, in all likelihood, a ceremony held at the special residence of the Kikoe Ogimi within the castle, and was intended to spiritually conquer the gods of the enemy country.

The Ubusuna-gami 産土神, god worshiped at the time of the First Sho dynasty, was Tsukishiro (the human manifestation of the god of the moon.) Therefore one might suspect that the above Omoro poem belongs to that period. However, that might not be the case if we judge from historical examples.

For instance, when Hojo Yasutoki 北条泰時 (1183~1242,) who was a regent of the Kamakura Shogunate, concluded the Joei Code of 1232 with an oath to the gods. This oath, which invoked the guardian deities of the region, was later adopted unchanged by the Tokugawa Shogunate in the 1600s. Therefore it is possible that the deity Tsukishiro, the human manifestation of the moon god, which was native to that region and connected with the First Sho dynasty, continued to be used and sung in ritual poetry under the Second Sho dynasty.

There is also an old orally transmitted teaching that there was a tradition of keeping a set of armor was at the residence of the Kikoe Ogimi High Priestess. Therefore it is reasonable to think that this ceremony was performed at the time of the Yaeyama expedition in 1500, and that it represents a ritualized form of the armed departure that had been practiced from the warring *Sanzan*, Three Mountain Kingdom, period (1314~1429) into the era of the First Sho dynasty (1406~1469.)

Other Omoro songs also celebrate overseas expeditions of that time, and they likewise contain phrases describing the divine majesty and authority of the High Priestess who protects the entire army.

Below is one example, a song describing the triumphant return from a military conquest (Book II, Chapter 30)

O Kikoe Ogimi, High Priestess
The army you lead
Resounds throughout the world with aweing all
The army led by
A noble lady

Ah, beloved lord,
Advance and survey the islands

Ah, beloved lord,
Advance and survey each foreign land

Guardian warriors,
Advance toward the foreign lands

Great Bushi,
Advance toward the foreign lands

Brave men,
Advance across all the islands.

Those on the road,
Return quickly

Generals,
Return with upmost haste

In summary, the song means:

The army being sent forth by the Head Priestess shines with the authority and glory of the king's domain. The army led by this supreme woman has made the glory of the king's country shine forth.

Beloved lord of the southern wind, go forth, attack the islands, conquer them and return.

Beloved lord of the southern winds, go forth and conquer the nations and return.

Warriors and fighters, unite your strength and attack the islands, then return.

Brave men of ferocious strength, be of one mind and conquer all the countries. Warriors aboard ships, attack the islands and return. Brave men of ferocious strength on every ship, make war and return home. Then they returned, their fame resounding even to the heavenly realm, they fought and came back victorious.

Around the same time there was also a sixty-two-line *Ayago* (a type of poem) which sings of how Sorabiro, the chieftain of Miyako Island, defeated Onitora "Devil Tiger" thereby capturing Yonaguni Island. The end of that poem contains the following lines.

If there is still war to be waged, I choose the time and set out
We go to greater Yaeyama or the surrounding Yaeyama islands

First we complete the great and fierce war rites,
We dance the dragonfly dance and the butterfly dance,

Then my forces attack, those in the front ranks strike down hundreds,
Those in the rear ranks sweep down hundreds more

Next we advance to the island of Yonaguni,
Encountering the lord of Yonaguni, the man known as Devil Tiger,

He steps forward, standing to face our forces,
His forces spanning across the entire sky,

The power of the chieftain spread as far as the eye could see.
Even if he looks back or tries to retreat, there is no escape,

Devil Tiger issued a challenge, "Very well, attack me then!"
To which I replied, "Face my longsword named Chigane Maru!"

Before my words were even finished,
My sword swept through Devil Tiger,

As easily as uprooting a yam,
The island, now pacified, flourishes

So the commander chose the right moment for battle and invaded Yaeyama. Before beginning the siege, priestesses performed the ritual butterfly dance and dragonfly dance. The soldiers in the front swept down the enemy, soldiers in the rear swept down the enemy. Finally, at long last, they began their advance on Yonaguni island. Once there they encountered Devil Tiger who controlled the farthest reaches of Yonaguni. He rose to confront them, saying "Come general of enemy forces, face me!" To which the reply was, "Then you shall face my great longsword, Chigane Maru (Golden Rule)!"

The moment those words were spoken, Devil Tiger was cut down instantly, as if slicing through a banana. As the army had been blessed by good fortune, peace was brought to the island and the army celebrated victory

首里のおきやかもいかなし天の御代に[illegible]金丸[illegible]

夏有寶劍神仙託曰號治金丸王稱真珠也　欽奉尊命雖不刻銘功名立碑

聖君之朝必有感化之祥瑞矣　恭見大琉球國

尚真王風來亂世崇賢出關功業於邦織於仁恕於士庶齊鳥之翼不相渝矣

昔年雖天發祖察度三代以後其餘世主雖遷化不用同行其以後百年以來男女殉道

周行喜救及二三十人矣以下人民五人三人應分齊死去仙家回非近依也

當君曰朕惟此道出夷也不可用之　聖母入滅日於國家具禁過焉

容惟道道貴安樂朕等并救人民豈勞是當君志急自急他救危扶傾有情爲先

當而不聽我而能抛踏大嶺北臣尊君子孝親弟隨兄欲老愛幼而已

大明嘉靖元年壬午十二月吉日　住山國[illegible]仙岩叟誌記之

Translator's Note: ***Inscription Praising the King's Virtue***

Rubbing of Koko Shotokuhi 国王頌徳碑 *Inscription Praising the King's Virtue* which was erected in 1522. The stone was destroyed in the battle for Okinawa in 1945 however pieces are in museums in Naha and a replica is in Shuri.

Image from:
Nihon Meihitsu Zenshu 日本名筆全集 Volume VIII 1931
By Irida Seizo 入田整三 (1885~1946)

While obviously we must read this while keeping in mind it is a tale of military conquest, we can note there was an old tradition of women being part of the vanguard.

Shortly thereafter, the famous sword Chigane Maru was presented to King Sho Shin and the circumstances of this are recorded in the stone monument titled *Inscription Praising the King's Virtue* (Koko Shotokuhi 国王頌徳碑,) erected in the first year of the Jiajing era of the Ming dynasty (1522.)

The main purpose of this engraved monument is to proclaim the prohibition of Junshi (following one's lord in death,) but in its preface it contains the following lines,

> During the reign of *Shuri Ogiya Kamoiganashi*, God-King of Shuri (this is Sho Shin's divine name,)[22] the sword Chigane Maru was brought from China. It became a sacred object imbued with divine spirit, and its praise is carved into this stone,
>
> > Here there is a treasured sword, an immortal being delivered an oracle, thereby naming the blade Chigane Maru. It is as smooth as jade and shines bright as pearls. It reverently obeys the command of the king.
> >
> > It was engraved with record of its merits and a monument erected. It is said that it will cause auspicious clouds to appear if the ruler is wise and just.[23]

Before this, King Sho Shin (1465~1527) carried out a policy of centralization, ordering the local lords (Aji) to reside in Shuri, which brought peace to Ryukyu.

As a result, the need for maintaining a military diminished, and a weapons throughout the land were confiscated. This is recorded in an inscribed stone erected within Shuri Castle in 1509 (the 4th year of Hongzhi in the Ming dynasty,) known as the*, Inscription on the Stone*

---

[22] *Ogiyaka* 於義也 Refers to King Sho Shin
Kamoiganashi 嘉茂慧 God intertwined with King, God and King as one.

[23] This is a quotation within a quotation. The first half of this inscription is in Ryukyu style Japanese and the second half is in Kanbun, the Chinese writing style used in Japan.

Railing of the Castle of the Hundred Bays,[24] (the stone contains eleven virtues of the king.) It states,

> Great care is taken to amass clothing, brocades, and utensils of gold and silver. Swords, halberds, bows and arrows are gathered in to serve as instruments for safeguarding the state.
>
> The resources and military equipment of this realm are beyond that which other provinces possess.

As the policy was to collect all weapons, the sword Chiganemaru was also likely presented to the court of King Sho Shin. Thereafter, the sword was passed down and preserved within the Sho royal family. According to an evaluation by the late Okakura Kakuzo, this sword was quite famous and is mentioned in several Omoro songs that describe it as *Reiken* a sword of divine provenance and supernatural powers.[25]

Furthermore, the *Record of Oshima Island* (Written in the twelfth year of Horeki (1762,) when a Ryukyuan oared vessel drifted ashore at Oshima in Tosa Domain. The author, Tobe Yoshihiro, interviewed one of the men on the boat named Shiohira Pechin and wrote down what he learned.)

He records,

> As a precaution against unforeseen foreign threats, all weapons have been collected and stored in the government offices.

Also,

> Long swords, short swords, spears, and other weapons were formerly imported from Japan, however they are not worn on a

---

[24] *Momourasoe Rankan no Me* 百浦添欄干之銘 The term "Castle of the Hundred Bays" is another name for Shuri Castle.

[25] *Reiken* 霊剣

Okakura Kakuzo 岡倉覚三 (1863 ~ 1913) Japanese scholar and art critic. Author of the English book, *The Book of Tea: A Japanese Harmony of Art, Culture, and the Simple Life* (1906)

> daily basis. They are worn on occasions such as a procession or other ceremony for a high ranking official. It is said that the inspection of swords and other weapons are carried out separately.

From this, we can understand that the weapons that were confiscated were preserved in case they were needed. At any rate, it seems there was absolutely no fear of internal revolt, nor was there any need to prepare defenses against a possible foreign invasion.

At the entrance to the harbor of Naha, two defensive batteries had been constructed. The southern stronghold, known as Yarazamori Castle, was constructed in the thirty-third year of the Jiajing era (1554) in China. In other words, it was built in the later years of King Sho Sei (1497~1555), the son of King Sho Shin (1465~1526.) There is a stone commemorating the construction of this castle carved with Ryukyuan Japanese recording the circumstances of its construction. At the end is the passage,

> As the need for defense against foreign lands diminished, weapons were collected and stored by the government.

It also notes that swords were sometimes carried to Japan or stored in Satsuma. This suggests that the confiscated weapons were not simply discarded, but were preserved by the royal government and used when necessary.

Later, during the reign of King Sho Nei (1564~1620), three artillery batteries were established, including the southern battery. At that time, an inscription composed in the Ryukyuan style concludes with the following passage,

> Under the firm rule of the Kikoe Ogimi, Okinawa was peaceful, and there had been no wars since ancient times. Even so, to proper governance dictated the country must protect its ports, so preparations were made. Should some crisis arise, the royal castle at Shuri would be defended first.
>
> Naha was also to be defended, and the regions of Shimazoe, Ozato, Chinen, Sashiki, Shimo-Shimajiri and Kyan each had their own defenses.

Yarazamori Gusuku 屋良座森城 Yarazamori Castle

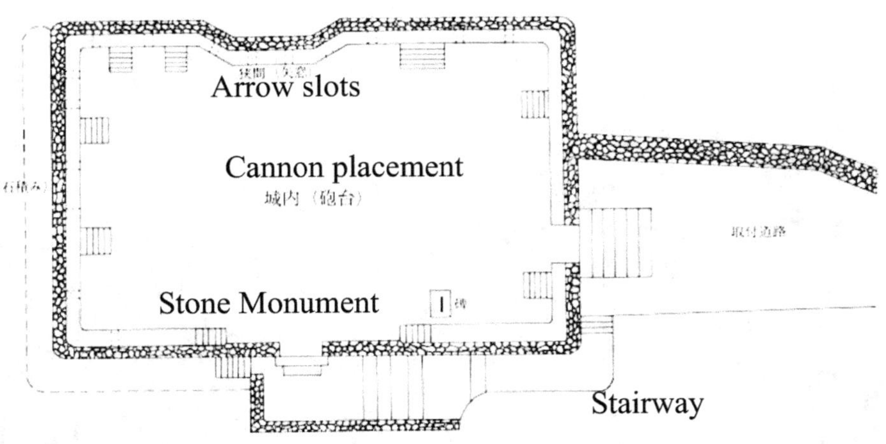

Yarazamori Gusuku **屋良座森城** Yarazamori Castle

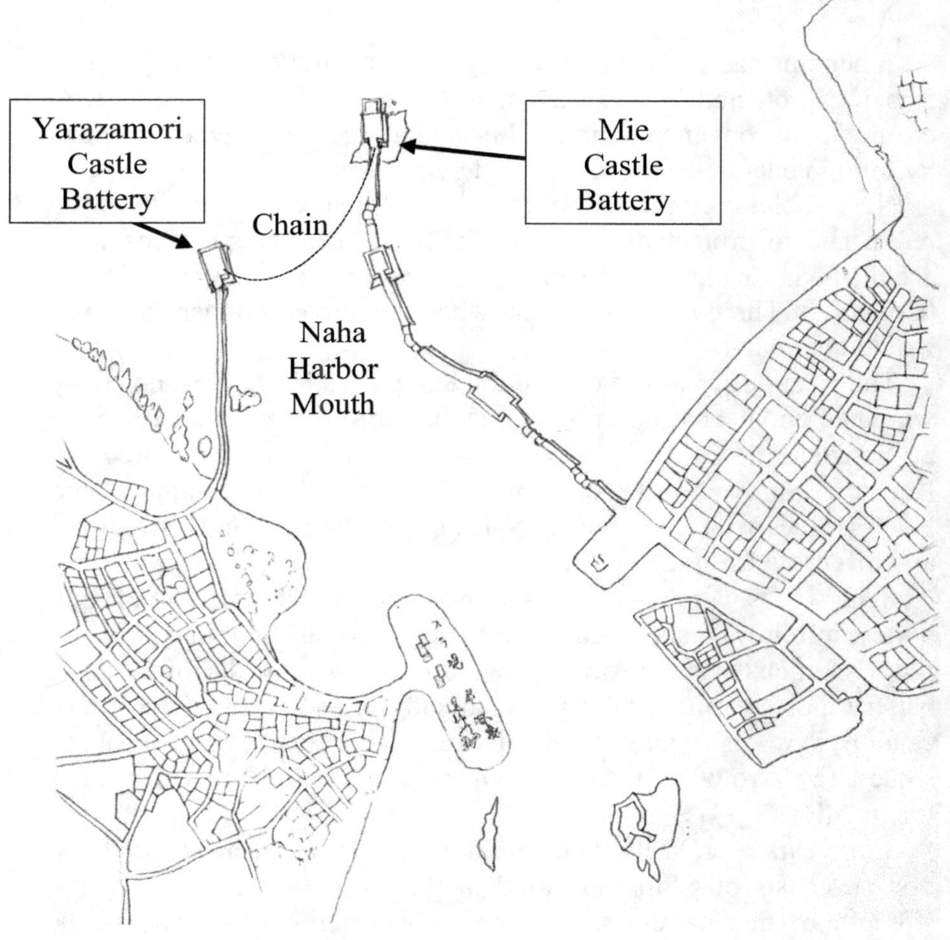
Yarazamori
Castle
Battery
Mie
Castle
Battery
Chain
Naha
Harbor
Mouth

The inscription continues,

> At Kakinohana and Yarazamori Castle, forces were gathered together. These orders were given by the royal court and were passed down throughout the islands, where they were firmly established.

When this passage is interpreted, it means that the land of Okinawa is being protected by the august virtue of the Kikoe Ogimi, who ensured that from ancient times, this land has never suffered invasions by foreign enemies or been troubled by pirates.

Nevertheless, by the will of the king, to ensure the security of the realm and to protect its ports and harbors, security measures were established. In times of emergency, the Three Councilors of State (Council of Three Chief Ministers who were directly under the King) would command.

The First Army would defend the King's castle, the Second Army would defend the harbor of Naha and the Third Army would assemble at Yarazamori Castle in Kakinohana, together with the forces of Haebaru, Shimazoe Ozato, Chinen, Sashiki, Shimo-Shimajiri and Kyan (forces from the ancient Nanzan, Southern Mountain region,) and offer loyal service.

Such words were regarded as an iron law. As there was an official policy, it follows that the armies were not to act rashly or in confusion. Since cannons were positioned within the stone walls of a castle battery indicates that artillery was already in use at this time. These cannon were also called Shima Kuzure Ishi Hiya "Island-breaking stone fire-arrows," meaning weapons capable of shattering fortifications.

Two years later, Wako Japanese pirates who had been attacking the eastern coasts of China appeared in the bay. However, due to the strength of this battery they were swiftly annihilated. Thereafter, peace continued for some time, until, half a century later, in the fourteenth year of Keicho (1609), the Satsuma forces invaded.

According to the *Diary of Shipmaster Kagesaku of the Seven Islands* [26] who accompanied the Satsuma army, the people of Tokunoshima resisted,

> The peasants all armed themselves with wooden poles that had been sharpened. Some attached knives to the end of bamboo poles or tied woodcutter's hatchets to them. Despite knowing they would be cut down they enter the fray and managed to cut down six or seven men from the Shonai division.
>
> Many were seen to flee to the ocean and were cut down on the shore. When the peasants attempted to make a defense, the Shonai troops, led by Shibue the Guardian of Tanba, advanced. They fired matchlocks, which pierced through their breastplates, and many men were struck down.
>
> Though scarcely visible to the eye, fire-arrows seemed to issue from the tops of the poles the men from Shonai held, striking the islanders down. Many ran into their houses but all were killed in the end.[27]

The section on Okinawa contains the following passage,

> Next, the Satsuma forces entered Naha harbor.The general along with the head warriors of the seven Tokara Islands assembled aboard ships from Tokara and led the initial assault.
>
> The entrance to the harbor of Naha was 25 Ken, 150 feet, in

---

[26] "Of the seven islands" refers to a resident of the twelve Tokara Islands, only seven of which were inhabited.

[27] "Further opposition was encountered when the Shimazu … landed on Tokunoshima. They arrived on 24 April and advanced … On 26 April, they went into the mountains on a manhunt to seek out and kill the defenders who had regrouped there. Here the Shimazu encountered Ryukyuans under the command of the son-in-law of Jana Teido. Between 200 and 300 Ryukyuan soldiers died in the fierce battle for Tokunoshima…The Satsuma force rallied and again brought in firearms to achieve control…Some looting appears to have taken place inside the islanders' houses, where the Satsuma samurai met further resistance from peasants wielding hatchets."

-*Samurai Capture a King: Okinawa 1609*
Stephen Turnbull, Osprey Publishing, 2009

> width and extended 50 Ken, 300 feet in length. High stone walls had been constructed, with arrow-slits opened at intervals. Large artillery pieces called Large Stone Fire Arrows were positioned, iron chains were stretched across the bottom of the harbor, and watchtowers placed strategically, making the defenses exceedingly secure.
>
> The Ryukyu commander, Shana Oyakata, led thirty-three mounted soldiers. They raised the previously mentioned chain across the harbor, they brought their artillery to bear, and as a result the attackers were completely destroyed. It is said that not a single man among the Ryukyu defenders was wounded.

Thus, what this record tells is that although the Satsuma army sailed into the port with small firearms, the Ryukyuans defended their position with cannons, preventing the Satsuma forces from making landfall. The invaders therefore withdrew northward and attacked by way of Unten Harbor.

Following this victory, a celebration was held at the residence of the Kikoe Ogimi, head priestess. In the *Omoro Soshi*, collection of remembrances in the form of songs, (Written in the third year of the Tianqi era, 1623, Which is fifteen years after the invasion of Ryukyu by Satsuma Domain.) On line thirty-one of paragraph six is a passage describing how the sacred *Ikusa Seji*, spirit of war, was bestowed to inspire the warriors, who had been struck with fear by the advancing *Yamato Shimaizuko*, warships and Samurai of Yamato, and the *Maheboshiya no Kuhara*, imminent attack.

The ceremony, held by the high priestess, served to eliminate *Ayogauchihama Yowachihe*, doubtful hearts, and prevented *Kimo ga Uchihama Yohachihe*, loss of fighting spirit. [28]

Though the Satsuma force numbered only about three thousand, the Ryukyu kingdom was long unaccustomed to warfare, and was therefore swiftly defeated. They then were compelled to submit to terms at the castle. In the *Origin Record of Iheya Island*, it is states,

> Three years after coming under the control of Kagoshima, a divine revelation manifested itself at the various sacred sites and

---

[28] The words in italics are the sections of the Omoro Soshi emphasized by the author. It is a Ryukyu-style Japanese that seems to mix both languages.

halls.

This revelation appeared in the form of a long sacred text called the *Misezeru*. The text begins with,

> The oracles from *Nirai-seji* (the oracle of the spirits of the eternal realm) and *Kanai-seji* (the same meaning as previous,) which relate that the sacred domain of Yamato had been subjected *Maiboshani* (to brave warriors,) *Nadakoroni* (conquered,) and *Tarasarete* (had their lands laid waste.)

Interpreting the above passage broadly, it seems to indicate the people of Ryukyu were exhausted and the only recourse was to work together on agriculture in order to benefit the country.

Regarding the organization of Ryukyu's military, you will find an essay by me in *Historical Geography* titled *Regarding the Administrative Divisions in Old Ryukyu* and can be found in issues one and two of volume sixty-six.[29]

Since being placed under the rule of the Shimazu clan, the Ryukyuans completely lost their ability to use weapons. However, as there was considerable trade with China and the need to defend against raids by pirates very real, they did possess a small number of firearms. These large and small firearms were lent from Satsuma domain when dispatching tribute ships to China.[30]

Invariably, several days before the departure of the tribute ships, it is said that the Ryukyu men practiced gunnery with all their might.

---

[29] *Historical Geography* 歴史地理
Regarding the Social Divisions in Old Ryukyu
古琉球のひき制度について

[30] Illustration of archery and gunnery practice on the following page from *Various Tales of the Southern Isles* by Nagoya Sagenta 1850.

大砲鍛錬図
川崎家の大砲南・侍
位して其後南喜祖父傳を
継て今に島人ども鍛錬す
る事なり

Also, they also practiced with *Fu-ya Kija-ku-* a type of explosive projectile. These consisted of unglazed earthenware pots packed with gunpowder with nail-like bits of metal that had three points, were packed in great quantities. The bombs would be thrown at pirate ships that approached, causing them to be engulfed in flames. This is probably a standard technique of using a earthenware pot to light a ship's sail on fire.

There are many engraved stone monuments that speak of ships being attacked by pirates in the seas around China. One such attack happened, according to the Western calendar, in 1805 (the fifth year of Kakei, in China.) As a tribute ship was making its way to China, it came under attack from several pirate ships. A detailed story of how the pirates were repelled with firearms and explosives can be found in *Record of the Mission to Ryukyu* by Ri Teigen.[31]

This ends my brief outline to the changes in military preparedness in Ryukyu, now I would like to discuss, as the title of this paper indicates, the development of Karate in Ryukyu.[32]

Although my theory have some errors in it, I believe that Karate must have developed in inverse proportion to the decline of the nation's military preparedness.

As the word "Karate" suggests, it was originally a form of Kenpo boxing transmitted from China. In earlier times, it was generally referred to as *Ta-u-de*[33] (generally speaking, most people simply referred to it as *Te*, hand.) This term may be derived from *N-Nachi-Kara-Te*, Weaponless and Empty Handed[34] but in more recent years the Kanji combination "Empty Hand" has come into regular use. These are *Ateji*, Kanji that represent the phonetic sound of a word.

Ryukyu first established trade with China in the early Hongwu period (1368~1398) of the Ming dynasty. It would not be unreasonable to surmise that it was during this era when Chinese Kenpo was introduced. However, during the late Ming period, when Ryukyu people were unable to carry so much as a *Suntetsu* for defense, they would have been very interested in such a method.[35]

---

[31] 使琉球記李鼎元 Ri Teigen (1750~1805)

[32] The author writes Karate all in Hiragana as からて

[33] The author writes this as: Ta た U う De で

[34] Kanji are 無手唐手 with the reading in Katakana ンナチカラテ

[35] Ming Era 1368 ~1644

Translator's Note: *Suntetsu* Iron Ruler

寸鉄

Illustration of a *Suntetsu* Iron Ruler

These were roughly 10 inch iron rods with a finger loop. They could be used to press into vital points or increase the effectiveness of joint locks. As they were easy to make, they were popular self-defense tools.

It would be reasonable to suppose that, in particular, those who went on tribute missions and stayed for two or three years at the *Juen-eki* (the Ryukyuan residence) in Fujian, China while engaging in trade, learned Chinese Kenpo as a means of self-defense and brought it back with them. My grandfather himself, for instance, made several journeys to Fujian and studied Chinese Kenpo while he was there, however as he considered it nothing more than a method of self-defense he never breathed a word about it.

According to the accounts of old people, in China there were few masters of this art among military officials, rather such masters were more common among merchants. Indeed, this makes sense. For those who constantly carried weapons, Kenpo was not particularly necessary, whereas Kenpo was indispensable for merchants who did not carry so much as a *Suntetsu*, iron ruler.

In Ryukyu, however, where people carried fans instead of swords, officials and merchants alike, irrespective of status, competed to acquire more learning. Before long it became widely popular, eventually even transforming how brawls were fought. There, regardless of social class, Samurai, Farmer, Craftsmen or Merchant, masters of Karate were called Bushi. This, of course, is using the Japanese word Bushi, warrior, and applying it to someone from any social station. From this we can glimpse changes in the social system.

Since the warrior class disappeared after the Satsuma invasion of Ryukyu, it was only natural that the word Bushi came to refer to a master of Karate. The term itself is, of course, borrowed from Japanese, and derives from a line in an *Omoro* song mentioned earlier concerning the invasion of Ryukyu.

Specifically it is the word *Bosha* from the line *Mahe Bosha*. Bosha is a local pronunciation of Bushi, warrior. Even today, the word Bushi is sometimes pronounced *Bushaa*. The prefix *Mahe* (pronounced Mae in Japanese means "front") is an honorific.

However, this term was probably used only in expressions such as *Yamato Mahe Bushaa*, Revered Warrior From Mainland Japan, and may not have been deeply integrated in the Ryukyu language.

In *Omoro* poems, there are many words that mean Bushi, or warrior, such as *Ma-bito*, *Gerahe Ma-bito*, *Koro*, *O-Koro*, *Nade Koro*, *Ma-Goro*, *Kainade Ma-Goro* and *Moriyaheko* as well as others.

(*Chikudun*, a word referring to a lower class Samurai, originally meant Bujin, one who studies the way of the warrior. I discuss this in my paper *Regarding the Social Divisions in Old Ryukyu*)

Korea
Honshu
China
Jeju Island
Fukuoka
Saga
Hakata
Dazaifu
Ōita
Fukue
Nagasaki
Kumamoto
Shikoku
Kyushu
Kagoshima
Satsuma
Tanegashima
Hirota
Yakushima
Tokara Islands
Amami Oshima
Kikai Island
Asama
Tokunoshima
Amami Island Group
Okinawa Main Island
Mugiya-higashi
Kagoshima Prefecture
Shuri
Taiwan
Miyako
Yaeyama
Nagahama
Ikema
Ōgami
Hirara
Tarama
Hatoma
Kohama
Yonaguni
Ishigaki
Hateruma
Taketomi
Okinawa Prefecture

At any rate, there is other strong evidence that the martial art known as Karate developed after the invasion of Ryukyu by Satsuma Domain. I once visited the principal islands of the Amami island group. Specifically Amami Oshima, Tokunoshima, Okinoerabu and Kikaijima. On these islands, not only does Karate seem to never have existed, but even when the people of these islands fight, they do not strike with their fists the way people of Okinawa do. While they do make a closed fist, they hit with the underside of it, and do not know how to strike with the protruding joints of the knuckles as Okinawans do.

In the Kaei era (1848~1854) a Samurai from Satsuma Domain named Nagoshi Sagenta wrote *Various Tales of the Southern Isles*. In his book he has two interesting illustrations depicting martial arts training. One shows *Tsukunesu*, the Ryukyu way of saying Kenpo Jutsu, and the other one shows Makiwara. However, these seem to have been practices later generations of merchants learned and trained, but not an art that ever became widespread among the general populace of Amami. Therefore, their way of brawling is entirely derived from mainland Japan.[36]

[36] Illustrations on this and the following page from *Various Tales of the Southern Isles by* Nagoya Sagenta 1850

拳法術
ソクチス
トツクロウ

In all likelihood, prior to the Keicho era (1596~1615) Okinawans were probably fighting in much the same manner as the people of Amami Oshima. However following the invasion by Satsuma in the fourteenth year of Keicho (1609,) Amami Oshima was separated from its mother country and placed under the direct control of the Daimyo of Satsuma Domain.

At any rate, when examining Okinawan culture, Amami Oshima serves as a useful point of reference for determining whether something originated before the Keicho period or developed after the invasion. For this reason, even in my studies of language, I always keep Oshima in mind as a basis for comparison.

There is little room for doubt that Karate truly began to develop in the years following the Keicho Era. Following the end of the Keicho era in 1615, while of course there were no wars in the Ryukyu islands, the people still brawled with each other and, in such situations, Karate was employed. While men who were particularly proud of their strength practiced it, children also began to instinctively strike each other with the knuckles of their closed fist when quarrelling. Thus it goes without saying that the art spread rapidly throughout the entire island chain.

Interestingly, there is a connection with the spread of Karate and Okinawan Sumo. The way Sumo wrestling is done is the same in both the Okinawan islands and on the Amami islands, however it differs in character from that of mainland Japan. It appears that Sumo underwent no change either before or after the Keicho period.

The reason Sumo remained unchanged while other martial arts underwent such changes is that the latter was not something created locally, but rather something introduced from outside. As stated in the well-known *Notes From Oshima* published in 1762,[37]

> Some years ago, there was a man named Kusanku who had a profound knowledge of Kumiai Jutsu,[38] (the author of this book,

---

[37] According to *Notes from Oshima* 大島筆記 by Tobe Yoshihiro a Ryukyu ship bound for Satsuma Domain encountered a storm and drifted until it shipwrecked in Tosa Domain. Tobe's book consists of a description of these events and interviews with the fifty-two crew members, including Ryukyu Shiohira Pechin Seisei 潮平親雲上盛成

[38] Kumiai Jutsu 組合術 "Paired Training Technique" refers to Kenpo.

> Yoshihiro Tobe says Kusanku learned it from the *Bubishi.*) Kusanku (this is said to be an honorific title, not his name) brought many disciples with him to Ryukyu from China.
>
> His techniques involved using both hands. One hand he would hold against his breast, while he executed techniques with the other hand. An aspect of particular note was his effective use of his legs and feet.
>
> Despite being an extremely thin and frail looking man, when a man of great strength seized him roughly, he was able to throw his opponent down or otherwise subdue him.

This was witnessed by the scholar-official Shiohira Pechin Seisei. It must have occurred seven years before the Ryukyu boat which was supposed to go to Satsuma domain drifted ashore in Tosa Domain.

This was around the time Sho Boku (1739~1794) was officially recognized as king by envoys from China in the *Sakuho*, investiture ceremony. Sho Boku was recognized as king in the twenty-first year of Qing Qianlong according to the Chinese calendar (In the Japanese calendar this is the sixth year of Horeki or 1756 according to the Western calendar.)

Kusanku probably heard that Kenpo was flourishing in Ryukyu and traveled from China in order to promote the art. It seems that the word "Karate" is actually a phonetic corruption of how Kusanku's name was pronounced *Kuushann Kuu.* It is important to note that long ago Karate was called *Kumiai Jutsu*, Paired Training Technique.

When speaking of showing a Karate Kata, the term *Tetsuka Yun* 手使ゆん is used. Further, the word *Maikata* 舞い方 Way to Dance, began with the word *Aimai* 相舞 Paired Dance. In other words it is a dance style that *Te wo Tsukau* 手を使う "Uses the Hands." As you dance, you look for an opening in your opponent and topple him. Nowadays this dance is done in many Inaka, local areas, and is also referred to as *Saa Saa Te* サーサー手 Saa Saa Technique. Thus it seems that even in traditional Ryukyu dance the influence of Karate can be found.[39]

---

[39] Illustration of Sumo on the following page from *Various Tales of the Southern Isles by* Nagoya Sagenta 1850

島人相撲之図

拳法研此二說

拳

茅子曰陳思王豪于文者也而其自敘手搏吉戯津津乎今之介弁反耻而不言嗟哉未之難已知點畫而後可以教八法知穰鞍而後可以教馳驟拳之謂也次其說于左

紀效新書曰拳法似無預於大戰之技然活動手足慣勤肢體此爲初學入藝之門也故存之以備一家學拳要身法活便手法便利脚法輕固進退得宜腿可飛騰而其妙也顚番倒插而其猛也披

In Volume Ninety of Bo Genki's *Bubishi* 武備志 *Treatise on Armament Technology* compiled in the late Ming Era, he writes the following preface to the section on Kenpo,[40]

Bo Genki (Mao Yuanyi) says: Chin Shio (Chen Si Wang) was a man of refined literary talent. Fortunately in his own writings he describes *Shuhaku*, unarmed fighting.[41] His description is eloquent and engaging! These days, however, those who pride themselves on rhetoric speak in a vulgar manner, this is lamentable! They do not yet understand the difficult underlying concepts of this art. You can only truly begin to learn this method after understanding these intricacies. It is only after you have gained a knowledge of the fundamentals and how to compare and assess can you be taught free application.[42] This is what is meant by Ken, fist or the art of unarmed fighting.

Looking to another source, in the *New Treatise on Military Efficiency*[43] Seki Keiko (Jixiao Xinshu) states:

> Unarmed fighting may seem to have little importance in large-scale warfare, however, training how to employ your hands and feet means your whole body becomes used to movement, and this is an important first step for those beginning training in the warrior arts. Therefore, they are preserved as fundamentals by teachers of this art.

---

[40] Previous page is the first page of the introduction to Kenpo.

[41] *Shuhaku* 手搏 Kanji are hand + to strike.

[42] The author seems to be saying, "Study the fundamental (Kata) before moving on to Randori, free sparring."

[43] *Jixiao Xinshu* 紀效新書 *New Treatise on Military Efficiency* is a 1560 military manual by general Seki Keiko/ Qi Jiguang. The *Bubishi* reproduces many sections of the *New Treatise*.

Seki Keiko defended against raids by Japanese Wako pirates and was eventually being assigned to coastal defense. He augmented his manpower by training local villagers in military skills. Discipline in Seki's army was harsh, with the death penalty for those who retreated in battle.

To learn Kenpo, you must focus on developing agile body movements, moving your hands deftly, having stable yet light footwork and be able to properly advance and retreat. Your legs should be strong enough to enable you to leap and soar. The subtlety of this are lies in the techniques of breaking your opponent's balance, countering, toppling and suppressing your opponent. The ferocity of this art lies in strikes that penetrate and cut, and punches that swing in from the sides. The speed lies in the ability of practitioners to quickly seize their opponents and restrain them, moving so fast it seems they will shoot up into the sky. The softness and flexibility of the art flashes across like lightning.

Thus, the Thirty-two Stances were developed. If combined properly when facing an opponent you will invariably prevail. An opponent facing the inexhaustible adaptability and unfathomable subtlety of your art will think it of divine origin.

As the common saying goes,

俗云 拳打不知 是迅雷不及掩耳

俗にいう拳は打たれても知らずこれ迅雷の耳を掩うに及ばざるなり

When facing a Kenpo practitioner, you will find a strike comes without warning. It is like boom of thunder that erupts too swiftly to cover your ears.

In short this method neither focuses on drawing an opponent in, nor does it emphasizes blocking, instead each attack unifies both offense and defense in one move. As you have a wide variety of techniques and a thorough understanding of strategy, you are able to alternate between attacking the upper body and lower body freely, leading to victory.

The same Thirty-Two Long Fist Postures, developed under the reign of Emperor Taizu of Song (927~976 AD,) that were taught in ancient time, are still being taught today. There are also the Six-Step Monkey Boxing and the Four Boxing methods. Each set of techniques has its own name, though in reality they are largely similar and only differ in the details. Even today, some of the finest techniques are: the Wen family's Seventy-Two Movements, the Thirty-Six Locking Techniques, the Twenty-Four Discard the Searching Horse techniques, the Eight Flashes of Rice Mountain methods, and the Twelve Short Techniques.

Though the Eight Downward Strikes of Hongba techniques are

strong, they cannot achieve the cotton-like softness of short strike techniques. Among the other current well-known schools of fighting are the leg techniques of Li Bantian of Shandong, the grappling of Eagle-Claw Wang, the throwing of Zhang Qian, the striking of Zhang Bojing, the staff methods of the Shaolin Temple combined with the Qing-tian staff methods, the spear methods of Master Gun of the Club, and the boxing and staff of Ba Zi.

Though each has its strengths and teachings that it passes down, they lack something below, or lack something above. Each method enables its user to defeat an opponent, however the techniques are limited in scope.

However, if you were to study all these schools it would be as if you mastered the snake formation of Mt. Chang: If you strike the head and the tail responds. If you attack the tail and the head responds and if you cut the body and both the head and tail respond.[44] This is what is meant by having complete offensive and defensive strength, both upper and lower, which means there is no opponent you can't achieve victory over.

All methods, whether it is using the fists, a staff, a sword, a spear, a hooked-sickle spear, or shield techniques, all rely on the fundamental hand and body movements in Kenpo. The following section will include illustrated explanations with important points highlighted.

---

[44] This snake and the related technique are mentioned in Sun Tzu's *The Art of War,*

The skilled soldier should follow the example of the Shuai-Ran, the famous snake of Mt. Chang. If you attack its head, it strikes with its tail. If you attack its tail, it strikes with its head. And if you attack its body, it strikes with both head and tail. You asked me if any army can imitate the Shuai-Ran snake? I say it can! Although the people of Wu and Yue hate each other, if two of them are in the same boat caught in a storm they will help each other just as the left hand helps the right.

The Art of War
By Sun Tzu
Translated by James Trapp (2013)

Note: Mt. Chang 常山 is another name for Mt. Heng the northern mountain of the Five Great Mountains of China. There is no information regarding the great serpent *Shuai-Ran.*

Translator's Note: The Eight Principles of Yong

The *Eight Principles of Yong* are used by calligraphers to practice how to write the eight most common types of strokes in regular script. The Kanji 永 means "eternity" and is written with the eight fundamental brush strokes. Mastering these strokes will mean you have beautiful, balanced.

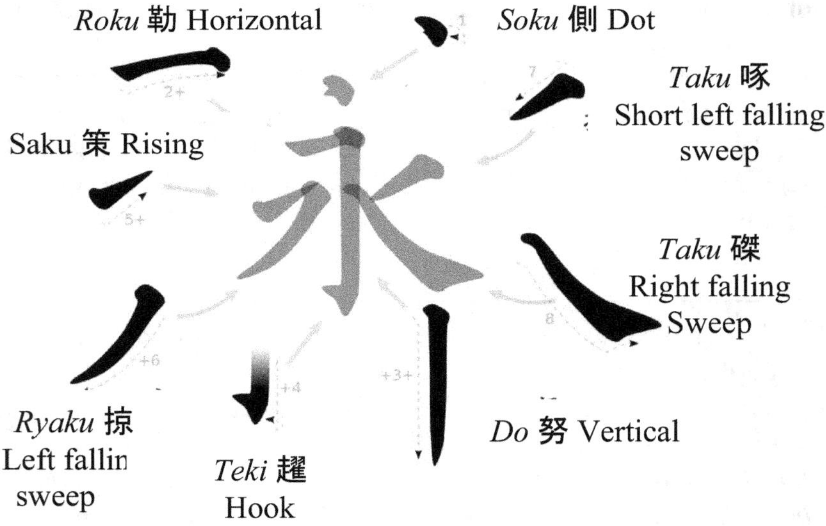

That ends the section on Kenpo in the Bubishi, *Treatise on Armament Technology*. Next I would like to highlight what General Seki writes in *The New Treatise on Military Efficiency,* [45]

> In calligraphy, you only proceed to The Eight Principles of Yong after learning how to draw the basic strokes and point that make up Kanji. Similarly, it is only after understanding how to sit firmly in the saddle should you be taught how to gallop. Therefore, I am introducing the Kenpo developed by Prince Si of Chen.[46]
>
> Although Kenpo may seem to have no connection to the strategies necessary to pit one great army against another, it nevertheless teaches how to manipulate your hands and feet and disciplines all parts of the body. In short it is the first gateway into the realm of martial training that you pass through at a young age. Therefore, it should be preserved and kept as part of the training within every military tradition.

This passage by General Seki is something that those who study Karate ought to adopt as a maxim to keep always at their side.[47]

The book goes on to explain the essentials of Karate,[48] briefly outlining this method, its history and schools. General Seki highlights the importance of study each of the schools, so that you can achieve *Shingi*, skills so advanced they seem of divine origin.

He ends the book by describing how in, particular, those who intend to study swordsmanship, spearmanship, archery and all other martial arts must first forge their every part of their body through Karate training. This conclusion almost makes it seem like he is predicting the worldwide spread of Karate.

It is interesting to note that within *The New Treatise on Military*

---

[45] *Jixiao Xinshu* 紀 効 新 書 (c1560s~1580s) By General Seki Keiko/Qi Jiguang 戚継光

[46] Prince Si of Chen is the posthumous name of Cao Zhi 曹植 (192 ~ 232AD.) Possibly referring to an early form of Tai Chi.

[47] *Zayumei* 座右銘 a favorite motto or saying. "Zayu" means to place an important book or item on your right hand side, where it is always within easy reach.

[48] The author is equating Kenpo to Karate.

Efficiency we can find such methods as Shorinji Temple *Kun* Staff Fighting and Qingtian *Kun* Staff Fighting. The word for staff or club 棍 is also pronounced *Kun* in Ryukyu, and these techniques have been practiced actively from ancient times.

Simply from seeing the word Kun, it is clear that both the word and the art was imported from China. That being said, nowadays this art has completely declined in urban areas and is only actively practiced in the countryside. There it is called Bo, wooden staff, and dancing while competing using it is called *Bo-odori*, wooden staff dance.

At any rate, that concept that a foundation in Karate is essential to learning all other martial arts is one I can nod my head in agreement to. However, whether this was actually carried out in its place of origin, China, is doubtful. Rather, it can be said that it developed among Ryukyu merchants and others who traveled to various regions in China and learned Karate as a method of self-defense. It seems likely that is was this group that succeeded in developing and refining Karate.

Thus it is hardly a coincidence that, following the decree banning weapons and their subsequent confiscation by the Ryukyu authorities, Karate became extremely popular. That being said, from long ago Karate training was done in strict secrecy. It was during this time that the motto,[49] *Karate ni Sente Nashi*, Karate never makes the first attack, originated.

Unfortunately, as the popularity of Karate spread, it began to take on a more *Musha-Shugyo-teki*, warrior training-like, aspect, which, for the sake of those on this path, something to lament.[50]

Nowadays, there are many schools of Karate, but they can be divided into two categories: Schools which basically remained Chinese Kenpo, and schools that have completely localized the martial art into something uniquely Ryukyuan. The former styles are mostly practiced in Naha, while the latter have chiefly flourished in Shuri.

Though there are considerable differences between these two types of schools it is impossible to simply state that one is superior and the

---

[49] The author uses the English word "motto" written as モットー

[50] By being more "warrior like" the author is perhaps indicating the art is shifting from one of self-defense to one used offensively in *Taryu jiai* 他流試合 inter-school fights/competitions, *Chikara Dameshi* 力試し tests of strength and so on.

other is inferior. That being said, it seems to me that the latter type of martial art has been adapted to better suit the physique of the people of Ryukyu. It seems clear that more research needs to be done in order to compare these two systems.

Mr. Funakoshi Gichin was truly the first person to introduce the latter system of Karate to mainland Japan, and through his martial skill and effort, this art is spreading throughout the whole country. This is surely not only a blessing for his native but the nation as a whole. This study was written in celebration of his sixtieth birthday.

www.ingramcontent.com/pod-product-compliance
Lightning Source LLC
LaVergne TN
LVHW020049110826
845155LV00029B/701